Original title:
A House of Many Voices

Copyright © 2025 Creative Arts Management OÜ
All rights reserved.

Author: Nathaniel Blackwood
ISBN HARDBACK: 978-1-80587-105-7
ISBN PAPERBACK: 978-1-80587-575-8

Narratives in the Night

Whispers dance like fireflies,
Chasing shadows, giggles rise.
Echoes of tales both old and new,
In corners where the secrets brew.

The cat's meow sounds like a chat,
While the dog plots against the rat.
The creaky stairs hold laughter's beat,
As stories tangle in loose retreat.

The Creak of Timeless Stories

The floorboards groan with ancient cheer,
As bedtime tales bring giggles near.
Each corner knows a punchline's wait,
While spirits dance and exaggerate.

A sock discarded tells a song,
Of laundry days that went real wrong.
The fridge hums tunes of midnight snacks,
In this realm, each mishap cracks.

The Festival of Forgotten Dreams

A hat on the lamp wears a grin,
While the curtains whisper, let's begin!
The clock strikes twelve, it's party time,
With chattering mice that can't keep rhyme.

A spoon playing drums with flair and zest,
And pillows hold gossip at their best.
Each dreamer hums a silly tune,
While the dust bunnies all dance in June.

Unspoken Bonds in Hidden Rooms

In the attic, stories wait to bloom,
Ghosts of laughter fill each room.
As books argue over who's the best,
And chairs debate where they should rest.

The wallpaper chuckles when it peels,
Revealing secrets like spinning wheels.
Beneath the floor, a napping cat,
Lazily guards the postman's hat.

The Dialogue of Generations

Grandma sings with a quacking tone,
While the toddler mimics, feeling grown.
Dad steps in with a dad-joke pun,
And Mom just rolls her eyes, having fun.

Cats on the windowsill share a stare,
But one just can't resist a daring dare.
With laughter bouncing off the kitchen walls,
It's a chorus of chatter, hear them all!

The Song of Resilient Walls

These walls have heard secrets and spills,
Like when Dad broke the door with his thrills.
Mom painted over with shades of cheer,
But the memories echo, ringing clear.

Neighbors' laughter leaks through the cracks,
While every nail's a tale that backs.
The kitchen's the stage for laughs on repeat,
And in the hallways, their rhythm's sweet.

Harmony in Loneliness

In corners where the dust bunnies play,
The walls hum softly, "We're here to stay!"
A solo sock dances all on its own,
While the fridge hums a tune, well-known.

The chair creaks a laugh, it's not really sad,
It's just tired from all the adventures it had.
Loneliness finds a quirky delight,
In shadows that dance, laughing at night.

The Narrative of Shattered Glass

Once there was a vase of great fame,
Now it's shards playing a new game.
With each piece telling a story bizarre,
Of the cat that leaped like a shooting star.

Each glint on the floor's a laugh from the past,
Echoes of chaos forever will last.
The broom sweeps up tales, both silly and grand,
While the dust loves the mischief, isn't life grand?

Echoes Within Four Walls

In corners, laughter bounces back,
A rubber chicken lost in a snack.
Socks debate who wears the best,
As curtains gossip, never at rest.

A dance of chairs, they clap and sway,
The fridge hums tunes to join the play.
Even the broom has its own beat,
As dust bunnies shuffle on tiny feet.

Whispers in the Hallway

The clock ticks tales of the day's events,
While doorknobs giggle, what fun it presents.
Shoes squabble, 'Who took the last step?'
As old lamps snicker, their light never crept.

Echoes of socks in a hiding chase,
Under the bed, they laugh at the space.
Walls lean in, eavesdropping with glee,
On the silly secrets of you and me.

The Many-Toned Realm

A symphony of clinks in the kitchen space,
The forks perform at an energetic pace.
Whisks and spatulas join in the fun,
As pancakes flip, their battle's begun.

In the living room, the cushions confide,
While the TV debates what to show next wide.
A jolly parade of mismatched socks,
Throw arguments that tickle like clocks.

Conversations in the Shadows

The shadows gather, plotting a prank,
On the unsuspecting couch, they thank.
A lamp throws light, then winks in delight,
As pencils argue who writes it right.

Curtains flutter, sharing a jest,
While the rug rolls over, "I'm the best!"
The windows whisper tales of the breeze,
As laughter escapes, knitting moments with ease.

The Chorus of Shadows

In the corner, whispers play,
Shadows dance at end of day.
One says 'Boo!' while others yell,
Echoes giggle, 'Can't you tell?'

A sock's in charge, it leads the show,
With rubber duck to steal the glow.
They laugh at feet that trip and slide,
As furniture joins in, quite pied.

Conversations in the Ceiling

Up above, the beams do chat,
About the cat, who's full and fat.
'Oh look, she sleeps!' the lamp will tease,
While cobwebs giggle in the breeze.

A cricket pipes a silly tune,
While dust bunnies boogie, oh how they swoon!
'Shh!' the rafters want more cheer,
As echoes croon, 'Is anybody here?'

Songs of the Forgotten Rooms

In closets deep, the coats conspire,
To make a band from lost attire.
A tattered scarf sings high and sweet,
While hats tap toes to the beat.

With shoes who guffaw and reminisce,
About the times they'd dance amiss.
A lullaby flows from under the bed,
As blankets shush the thoughts still fled.

Harmonies of Distant Memories

Old photos laugh from dusty frames,
Recalling wild and wacky games.
'Remember when we flew so high?'
The laughter rings as time slips by.

In the attic, an old toy sings,
Of childhood dreams and paper wings.
'Let's do the cha-cha!' echoes spread,
While night bears witness to fun long dead.

Shadows in the Corner

In the corner, shadows dance,
Whispering secrets, snatching chance,
A cat jokes with a broom's thin leg,
While a startled sock begins to beg.

The toaster sings of burnt bread woe,
While the curtains giggle, swaying slow,
Plates gossip about the dinner gone,
And the fridge hums a tuneless song.

Dust bunnies hold their annual fair,
With squeaky mice, they twirl in air,
Each room a stage, a laugh awaits,
As walls conspire, twisting fates.

In laughter's grip, we're intertwined,
Every nook's a story, misaligned,
So raise a glass, to spirits awake,
In this chaos, the best jokes break.

Portraits of the Unheard

In frames upon the wall they stare,
With painted grins, that fill the air,
Whispers sneak from their silent lips,
As the dog distracts with playful dips.

A wardrobe sways, boasting its wares,
While an old clock tells how time bears,
The couch holds tales of restless nights,
While shoes plot journeys, winged flights.

Lamps chuckle at the light they share,
Glowing softly, without a care,
Each knick-knack winks, a secret tease,
In this gallery, nothing's as it seems.

So gather 'round, all curious eyes,
For in this room, the laughter flies,
With tales unscrolled, just take a look,
At the portraits of the world in a book.

Layers of Echoing Souls

Beneath the floor, a chorus hums,
Echoes of laughter, then sudden drums,
A grandma's quilt tells stories grand,
While the papers flutter, lending a hand.

Each layer peels with a hearty cheer,
Ghosts of past dinners filling the sphere,
Echoes bounce from each creaky stair,
As the pets join in, unaware of despair.

Cracks in the walls weave tales divine,
Faint giggles from a lost bottle of wine,
In the basement, a piano decrees,
"Hurry up! Dance! Join the kitties, please!"

Every heartbeat, a tune to sway,
In this ruckus of souls, let us stay,
For with every burst of a joyful sound,
A wild tapestry of life is found.

The Unbroken Chain of Stories

Gather 'round the fire's warm glow,
Where tales zip by, like a swift crow,
Old Grandpa starts with a chuckling rhyme,
While the kids giggle, losing all time.

A pot clinks as the soup stirs dreams,
Each spoonful savored, laughter beams,
A noodle bends, spilling secrets anew,
Linking each story like a perfect brew.

The chairs sway as they strain to hear,
The tall tales told, embracing cheer,
Whispers fly like confetti's burst,
In this circle, we quench our thirst.

Hold tight to the threads, don't let them go,
For stories told carve paths below,
In laughter's embrace, the night thus ends,
With tales as bonds, where love transcends.

The Breath of Old Ashes

In corners where the dust has danced,
Old echoes giggle, slightly pranced.
A teapot chuckles, it's seen it all,
Stirring up trouble at the ghostly ball.

The fireplace grumbles with tales long gone,
While the armchair snores, then snickers on.
The curtains whisper of secrets spilled,
As mischief brews in the air, unfilled.

Memories That Speak in Color

Crayon walls boast of wild debates,
The fridge hums softly about dinner plates.
Giggling socks play hide and seek,
While the lamp blinks, trying to speak.

Spilled paint on the floor, a rainbow burst,
The cat curates tales, a furry first.
Walls adorned with laughter's frame,
Echoing stories, none the same.

The Distortion of Time

Socks on the line wave to the past,
Ticking clocks tickle moments that last.
The rug rolls its eyes at shoes that tread,
While the curtains flap stories long dead.

Dishes debate who was washed more,
As soap bubbles bubble with years to score.
Time takes a leap, then trips on a chair,
Turning memories funny, a laugh in the air.

The Gaps Between Words

Conversations are like jigsaw pieces,
Often missing some sprightly releases.
The toaster pops jokes, makes us smile,
While the kettle chimes in with style.

In silence, the fridge hums a sly tune,
As neighbors gossip beneath the moon.
Whispers hide 'neath the creaky floors,
The gaps between words dance out the doors.

Underneath the Roof of Reminiscence

In the attic, ghosts debate,
Old socks and hats join their fate.
A toaster hums a sleepy tune,
While the broom dances with the moon.

The walls whisper secrets of old,
Spilling tales that never get cold.
A potbellied cat, quite the sage,
Writes poetry on every page.

The floorboards squeak with laughter light,
As chairs gossip late into the night.
A cupboard hiccups, bursting with spice,
Mixes memories like they're rice.

In this haven of joyful din,
Where laughter echoes, and dreams begin.
Every corner holds a cheeky quirk,
Underneath the roof, where we all smirk.

The Murmuration of Voices Past

In the hallway, whispers swirl and twirl,
As the mirror cracks a knowing whirl.
The curtains plot a sneaky dance,
While the china performs its glance.

A clock ticks time not quite aligned,
As teacups share the tales they find.
An old sock puppet begs for a show,
Claiming he's the star, don't you know?

The lightbulb flickers, throws a wink,
While the old chair begins to think.
With a honk and a giggle, they proclaim,
This mirthful house knows no shame.

So gather near, embrace the jest,
In this lively nest, we're truly blessed.
Voices echo, a vibrant parade,
In this raucous ballet we've made.

The Tones of Yesterday's Dreams

Underneath the stair, a tune does hum,
A ukulele plays, though it's slightly dumb.
The fridge sings low, in an off-key tone,
Causing all the leftovers to moan.

With crickets chirping in the hallway's bend,
While mismatched socks plot their latest trend.
The wallpaper flutters, claims it's alive,
As dust bunnies laugh and take a dive.

The couch snoozes through the day's bright rays,
While the lamp shares stories from ancient days.
A playful echo joins this merry crew,
Crafting a soundtrack, just for you.

Here the quirks collide in silly ways,
Where dreams hang out and mischief plays.
So listen close, though it might seem strange,
Each sound a memory, waiting to exchange.

Rhythms of the Heartbeat

In the kitchen, pots and pans,
They sing together, clanging bands.
The fridge hums softly, a buzzing tune,
While forks and spoons are dancing soon.

Ceiling fans twirl, they spin around,
Whispers of laughter echo the sound.
Floors creak gently, a rhythm sweet,
Even the cat joins in on the beat.

Pillows gossip when no one hears,
Sharing secrets, laughing through tears.
In every nook, a chuckle resides,
A symphony where the heart abides.

Voices collide like colors bright,
Creating chaos, a joyful sight.
Every corner has a tale to tell,
In this lively place, all is well.

The Palette of Silent Exchanges

In the hallway, shadows prance,
A painting whispers, in a dance.
The chairs hold court with tales untold,
In a cozy nook, laughter unfolds.

Underneath the staircase wide,
Books converse, with secrets inside.
Dust bunnies giggle, avoiding a sweep,
A playful pact, their promise to keep.

The clock ticks on, a comedic show,
Chasing time as moments flow.
Windows wink at the sun's embrace,
As if they're sharing a sweet, warm space.

In a garden, daisies compete,
For the best joke, the funniest feat.
With each flutter, whispers ignite,
In this lively realm, all feels right.

Echoing Dreams on the Stairs

Whispers float up wooden steps,
Where each creak holds a secret, perhaps.
Laughter spills like a playful stream,
In the night, they chase a dream.

On the landing, shadows collide,
Chasing giggles they cannot hide.
Ghosts of memories twist and churn,
In the dance of the feet that yearn.

Light flickers on, a comical sight,
As ghosts share jokes in delight.
Echoing dreams bounce off the walls,
A spirited gathering that never stalls.

From room to room, the humor spreads,
As pillows converse on laughter's beds.
In every step, a quirk appears,
Chasing away all fearful fears.

The Abode of Lost Reflections

Mirrors chuckle with every glance,
Reflecting mishaps in a silent dance.
Each one holds a joke or two,
Of makeovers gone wrong, oh what a view!

In forgotten corners, dust motes play,
Casting shadows in a cheerful way.
Old shoes gather for a gala night,
Telling tales of the whimsical flight.

The wardrobe hums, a tune of delight,
Of outfits worn in the strange moonlight.
Hats tipped low, they nod and bow,
To memories fresh, like this jesting vow.

In this haven where laughter rings,
Even the walls have funny things.
Reflections swap their secrets sly,
In a haven where smiles never die.

Voices that Shape Our Existence

In the kitchen, pots begin to clatter,
The spoons all sing, and the cat's a chatter.
A toast to the ghost who loves to bake,
Whispers of sugar in every mistake.

Footsteps echo in the hall, oh my!
An old chair creaks with a friendly sigh.
Each laugh and jest fills the air with cheer,
As shadows dance, and we all persevere.

The fridge hums softly, its secrets in tow,
Announcing the pizza is ready, let's go!
While socks in the dryer hold debates so bold,
Who shrunk the towels? The story's retold.

Voices blend like a colorful stew,
In this lively circus, there's gold for you.
We argue and giggle, a rhythmic embrace,
In this cacophony, we all find our place.

Dialogues of the Heart

Two teacups chatter, their edges collide,
Spilling the tea and secrets inside.
The plants in the corner gossip about sun,
While clocks tick tock the day has begun.

A dog in the yard, with a bark that's sweet,
Shares tales of the mailman, who runs down the street.
The sofa is grumpy, its cushions astute,
It groans about guests and their rambunctious loot.

In the bathroom, the shower's a song,
Singing to shampoo that's been there too long.
The mirror reflects grins, some frowns, awkward glares,
As we practice our speeches, looking for prayers.

Through all the banter, we learn day by day,
Though voices may clash, they guide our own way.
In this quirky symphony, laughter and tears,
We build our own chorus that echoes through years.

The Unseen Gathering

In the attic, the dust bunnies start to scheme,
Whispering secrets, plotting a dream.
An old record player spins tales from the past,
As laughter lingers, its shadows are cast.

The walls are alive with a thrum and a hum,
A chorus of memories, hear the drum!
Chairs creak with delight, excited to share,
Old socks join in, with antics laid bare.

The cobwebs giggle, they've heard it all,
Of family feuds and that time we did fall.
While shoes tell the tales of journeys and trails,
The murmurs of history flow like fresh gales.

As the sun dips low, casting a glow,
Voices unite like a spirited show.
Here laughter echoes and joy holds tight,
In this unseen gathering, hearts feel light.

Soundwaves of Memory

Echoes of laughter bounce off the walls,
As cookies crumble and the old phone calls.
The doorbell rings, a surprise to delight,
Voices collide in the magical night.

In the backyard, the barbecue's a friend,
Sizzling sausages as the stories extend.
The grill has opinions, it sizzles with flair,
While comedians from last year compete for the air.

Pillow fights spark in the twilight glow,
With laughter that spirals and dances just so.
The popcorn pops, synchronizing the fun,
In this theater of memories, we joyfully run.

Even the clock on the wall joins the cheer,
Ticking along to the sounds that we hear.
With every burst of joy, it pulls us close,
In the soundwaves of memory, we love the most.

The Melodies of Fading Light

When shadows dance and giggles fade,
The fridge hums tunes we never laid.
Old chairs creak a silly song,
Where whispers tangle and belong.

A cat sings tales of clumsy fights,
While ceiling fans spin comical flights.
Laughter echoes down the halls,
As pizza boxes line the walls.

The clock ticks time with a playful tick,
Each second moves a little slick.
Ghosts of friends still roam and play,
In this funny, fading ballet.

So let the laughter roll like thunder,
As memories spin in playful wonder.
It's not just walls that hold the night,
But the giggles caught in fading light.

Hushed Conversations of the Past

In corners tucked, where voices giggle,
Old stories twist, and shadows wriggle.
A rubber duck just quacked a tune,
As whispers dance beneath the moon.

The table's secrets spill like wine,
As socks debate on who's divine.
A chair remarks, 'Oh, what a show!'
While the old rug snickers low and slow.

Fragrant moments hug the air,
With echoes of mischief everywhere.
In kitchen nooks, they sing and sway,
Those hushed talks weave their funny play.

Who knew that dust could hold such charm?
As memories jiggle without a qualm.
Each corner holds a silly jest,
And laughter's where the heart feels blessed.

The Canvas of Communal Silence

On walls adorned with laughter's grace,
A canvas bright, with a twist of face.
Mismatched socks have tales to share,
While quiet says, 'Do we dare?'

An empty room with echoes strong,
Recites the notes of joyful throng.
Candles flicker with a sassy wink,
As furniture nods, and walls all think.

The clock, a wise old sage, it seems,
Tick-tocks the laughter from our dreams.
Jars of jelly giggle on the shelf,
The sound of chatter lost in stealth.

In silence thick, the humor grows,
As sweet absurdity often shows.
A quirky place, where whimsy thrives,
This canvas hums with all our lives.

Resounding Moments in Memory

Once upon a time, or was it yesterday?
A donut whispered, 'Come out and play!'
Across a table set with cheer,
Moments bounce, they're always near.

A voice like thunder, a laugh like rain,
The pasta pot was full of pain.
A rubber band snapped, oh what a sight!
As friends just burst into delight.

Old shoes argue on where they've been,
As habit quirks dance on a whim.
Underneath the laughter's cover,
Memories twist, connect, and hover.

So gather round this silly space,
Where moments tickle and embrace.
In echoes loud, the fun remains,
Resounding laughter in our veins.

Revelations of the Everyday

In the kitchen, pots and pans,
Spoons join in a jolly dance.
Fried eggs flip, toast pops up,
While the cat plots, in a trance.

The quirky clock ticks out-of-time,
With a whir and a wheeze, it chimes.
The dog barks back, a splendid rhyme,
As I brew my morning prime.

A blender screams a blending tale,
Juicy fruits begin to wail.
The coffee pot whispers sweetly,
Caffeine dreams that never fail.

Dinner plates clash like old friends,
Forks and knives start their amends.
From salad woes to pie's great ends,
In each story, humor blends.

Cadence of Companionable Silence

In hush now, the fridge takes a breath,
Its hum a tune, a life beneath.
The sofa sighs as we both sit,
These quiet moments, perfectly knit.

The old lamps flicker with a grin,
Shadows dance, inviting kin.
Silence speaks, yet laughter looms,
As popcorn pops in varied tunes.

Outside, the squirrels hold a debate,
Chasing tails, they seal their fate.
A chuckle sneaks from behind the book,
In this calm, mischief likes to look.

Time slips by on this lazy eve,
Joyful both, we just believe.
In silence, every smile we weave,
With every blink, no need to leave.

Euphony of the Everyday

The broom sings softly as it sweeps,
Dust bunnies join in chorus leaps.
A mop taps lightly, keeps the beat,
While the duster twirls with nimble feet.

The vacuum roars a raucous song,
Chasing crumbs that do not belong.
Windows squeak in a high-pitched key,
As we laugh at echoes in glee.

In the bathroom, the shower croons,
Water splashes, a symphony looms.
The soap bubbles giggle and pop,
In this waltz, we all hop and bop.

Outside, the wind plays its flute,
Leaves rustle, a merry pursuit.
In every sound, a tale to tell,
In joy we dwell, as all is well.

The Soundtrack of Our Lives

The kettle whistles a whiny tune,
While laundry spins a folksy croon.
Dishes clack in a rhythmic dance,
Even socks join with a sly prance.

The doorbell jingles in a chirpy way,
Welcoming mishaps of the day.
Dings and dongs, oh what a sound,
As chaos narrows all around.

With every hiccup, each playful chime,
Moments melt in disastrous rhyme.
In this cacophony, we find mirth,
A soundtrack that hums right to earth.

As night descends, the crickets play,
A serenade to end the fray.
Together we laugh, in joy we bask,
In every note, a million tasks.

The Lullaby of Timeworn Spaces

In creaky halls, a ghost sighs,
The clock ticks loudly, no surprise.
Dust bunnies dance, they put on shows,
With squeaks and squeals, they steal the toes.

A cat ambles by, gives a knowing glance,
Chasing shadows in a silly prance.
The old chair creaks with every weight,
Whiskers twitch as if to narrate.

There's a sock in the cupboard, oh what a tale,
Of laundry day battles where few prevail.
Forks, spoons sing harmony in the drawer,
Every mealtime feels like a choreographed chore.

Whispers of yesterday bounce off the walls,
Finding old treasures hidden in stalls.
Lullabies of laughter echo all day,
In these timeworn spaces where kids come to play.

Voices Beneath the Roof

Under the rafters, secrets collide,
The squirrel and the mouse share peanut butter pride.
Each floorboard creaks under a chuckle,
As Uncle Fred tells tales that always buckle.

The fridge hums a tune, a dance of delight,
While the curtains gossip about the moonlight.
The kettle's whistle sings in high pitch,
Inviting all critters to gather and switch.

A family of hats hangs near the door,
Each with a story worth shouting for more.
They argue about who wore whom best,
While the slippers snicker, sensing the jest.

In this roof's embrace, laughter has wings,
Where every corner of home joyfully sings.
Voices mingle, each one a delight,
Creating a symphony, day turns to night.

The Palette of Intertwined Lives

In a kitchen painted with flavors galore,
The blender's a DJ—mixing up scores.
Spatulas clink like maracas in hand,
While aprons sway to the beat of a band.

The fridge holds a party, with leftovers loud,
A casserole chorus, forming a crowd.
An open cupboard, a curious sight,
Where mugs gossip softly about tea every night.

Stairs creak like sneakers in chaos and cheer,
As kids tumble down, bringing jokes we hold dear.
The bookshelf's alive with stories to take,
While bookmarks giggle, wishing for a break.

Each room a canvas, a vibrant display,
Where laughter and love weave through the day.
Intertwined lives, a colorful spree,
In the palette of home, you'll find harmony.

Secrets Whispered Through Vents

Under the floor, a raccoon will scheme,
Trading good gossip with a curious dream.
He tells the vacuum the juiciest plot,
As the dust bunnies giggle, connecting each dot.

The walls have ears, they hear every laugh,
As children debate who's better at math.
The windows throw shade at the passing cars,
Sipping sunlight like it's candy from Mars.

In the bathroom, the shower has tales to unfold,
As soap suds dance, bold and uncontrolled.
The toilet hums soft while holding its breath,
Waiting for secrets, life, and even death.

Through metal vents, the whispers will breeze,
Tickling the senses like a playful tease.
Every crevice, every nook, alive with delight,
Secrets are shared in the heart of the night.

The Language of Home

In the kitchen, pots do cheer,
While the fridge hums secrets near.
Cups chime in a merry tune,
As the spoons join in to swoon.

The sofa cracks a silly joke,
While the lamp begins to poke.
Dust bunnies dance a jig on floors,
As laughter bumps against the doors.

The clock ticks loud, a shuffling beat,
Whispers of snacks, a tasty treat.
Pets join in with woofs and purrs,
Their silly antics cause a stir.

Walls echo tales of ancient fights,
As curtains flutter in silly lights.
Together brewing a lively song,
In every nook, we all belong.

The Soliloquy of Space

Beneath the stairs, ghosts play hide,
While the old vacuum takes a ride.
Whispers float from the closet door,
As dust collects on the wooden floor.

The bathroom mirror takes a peek,
Hoping for a chat, so we speak.
The toilet whispers all it knows,
Of midnight snacks and bathroom woes.

Windows giggle at the rain,
As puddles form a dancing chain.
The ceiling laughs from up above,
With every thud, it sends us love.

In every shadow, stories swirl,
As space itself begins to twirl.
A giggling echo of our days,
In cozy corners where we play.

An Archive of Echoing Memories

Photos grin from the hallway wall,
Each smile a giggle, each pose a call.
Old shoes dance with a playful creak,
As they whisper secrets, cheek to cheek.

The attic hums with a curious tune,
Where toys once played beneath the moon.
Socks lose a battle, all alone,
Searching for partners, never known.

Books talk back with wisdom bold,
Tales of journeys sweetly told.
Their pages flutter in gentle breeze,
Sharing laughter and memories with ease.

Echoes linger, bright and clear,
Calling out the ones held dear.
In this archive, joy unfolds,
Every moment cherished, every laugh retold.

Tales Told by the Wind

Outside, the branches sway and grin,
As whispers of stories swirl within.
The mailbox keeps secrets, tucked away,
From letters that dance on a brightening day.

The fence creaks softly, sharing its lore,
Of hurried footsteps and laughter galore.
Rabbits gossip in the garden beds,
While the petals nod their sleepy heads.

Clouds overhead, a raucous crew,
Puffing up tales of skies so blue.
The breeze spins laughter across the way,
A merry tune to brighten the day.

Through every whisper, both soft and loud,
The tales on the wind draw in the crowd.
In this playful breeze, joy finds its flight,
A symphony sung from morning to night.

The Secrets We Share

In the attic, ghosts play cards,
Whispers scatter like falling shards.
A cat sings opera, off-key and loud,
While the dust bunnies form a proud crowd.

In the kitchen, spoons argue with forks,
The fridge hums tales of old jigsaw works.
Cookies giggle, hiding behind the jars,
While waffles chat about their missing czars.

Living rooms host debates with the couch,
The curtains gossip about each new pouch.
A clock chimes jokes in a tick-tock tune,
As laughter spills out like a bright balloon.

Under the stairs, the shoes have a ball,
Old flip-flops dance, the high heels stand tall.
With each clap, the echoes bounce off the wall,
Turning the house into a giant hall.

Harmonies Beneath the Roof

The ceiling sings in a creaky pitch,
While radiators hum—a warm little glitch.
A blender serenades in a swirling spree,
As the window flirts with a buzzing bee.

Dishes clash in a melodious clatter,
The rug rumbles, oh, what a chatter!
Lamp shades sway to the rhythm of light,
Balloons float with glee, so bright and light.

Laughter bounces like a wild rubber ball,
As sofas argue who's the best for a sprawl.
The television chimes in, a voice so deep,
Chasing the dreams that whirl in a heap.

In this playful chaos, all is well,
With every chuckle, a new story to tell.
Under one roof, in a fanciful mood,
Life's a concert, hilarious and crude.

Tapestry of Unspoken Words

Curtains whisper secrets from the sun,
While the floorboards groan about their run.
Pillows are judges, with soft, plush glee,
Deciding who's right in the great TV spree.

Dust motes twirl like dancers in space,
Tickling the nose of the old cat's face.
The wallpaper has tales of the past,
Of all the odd gatherings, the joy amassed.

Jars of cookies conspire in the night,
While spoons draft plans for a culinary flight.
Laughter ripples like a fresh, cool breeze,
Tickling the heart, putting minds at ease.

Voices mingle, like a quirky blend,
Where stories twist and troubles mend.
In the chaos, a symphony found,
With each quirky tune, laughter's abound.

Murmurs of the Past

Old photos grin from the dusty frames,
As memories play their silly games.
The fireplace chuckles at ghostly tales,
While the mantelpiece winks, it never fails.

A broom joins in on the sweeping fun,
With a creaky twist, it dances, it runs.
Chairs swap stories of who sat where,
As shadows leap, filling the air.

Footsteps echo of the kids at play,
Reliving adventures from yesterday.
The pantry snickers at missed midnight snacks,
While curtains uplift their old, dusty cracks.

In this symphony of voices and time,
Even the silence has a giggling rhyme.
Hidden in corners, there's laughter unfurled,
In this merry home, joy is twirled.

Symphony of the Silenced

In the attic, a cat sings loud,
While the old clock does a jig, proud.
A broomstick dances with a hat,
And the curtains sway like a friendly brat.

The fridge hums a tune of ice cream dreams,
The lampshades twist, it seems,
As the spoons in the drawer start to clink,
Conspiring to get that old man to blink.

The couch whispers secrets, it's got the scoop,
While the vacuum cleaner joins the loop.
Socks hold rallies in the laundry room,
Convinced they can escape their looming doom.

Even walls crack jokes, it's a merry affair,
Shaking with laughter, they float in the air.
Each echo a giggle, each creak a jest,
In this silly symphony, we're all blessed.

The Chorus of Forgotten Dreams

Beneath the bed, old toys convene,
Chatting about times when they were seen.
Dust bunnies strategize how to unite,
Hoping for a cleaning spree to incite.

A calendar whispers 'remember the day',
When socks made a run for the laundry bay.
The post-it notes join with sticky hand grips,
Planning a heist for some snicker-sweet trips.

The toaster pops up tales of burnt bread,
While the kettle quips, 'No more tea, I've fled!'
In shadows, whispers of dreams long gone,
Groan in delight as they spin on and on.

They're a raucous lot, this merry band,
Each forgotten story a treasure unplanned.
With laughter they lift the mundane each day,
Inviting us all to their folly-filled play.

When Walls Speak Back

When you say something, don't be so sure,
The walls might have riddles to endure.
A tap and a thud become wise replies,
Filling the air with their clever guise.

Each corner keeps secrets, each crack holds a tale,
Of chuckles and mischief, a curious trail.
They murmur of dinners, of spills on the floor,
Of moments so funny, we just can't ignore.

The painting winks, as the frames creak low,
Mocking our banter in the soft, eerie glow.
And when the wind howls, it carries a chuckle,
As if it's responding to a vague rustle.

So, next time you talk, don't feel alone,
Join in the chatter of your rather sweet home.
For in simple whispers, humor hangs tight,
Inside these four walls, laughter takes flight.

Reflections of Distant Laughter

In the mirror, giggles reflect back at me,
Showing old selfies with mischief and glee.
The shampoo bottles nod and they sway,
Recalling the fun in that wild, messy play.

Bathroom tiles hum a pop song so cool,
While the bath mat snickers, 'That's how you drool!'
The towel takes a bow, a comedic act,
Joining the laughter, it's a cozy pact.

Out in the hallway, shoes chatter away,
'Remember the time we ran out that day?'
The coat rack chuckles, holding its breath,
Spinning stories of life until death.

As dusk falls softly, the laughter entwines,
In the tapestry of memories, joy still shines.
So let all voices combine to create,
A melody of laughter we'll celebrate!

The Resonance of Old Stories

In corners lurk tales, both wild and grand,
A lost shoe dances, led by a hand.
Whispers of socks in a laundry mound,
Tell secrets of monsters who once were found.

A cat in a hat, a hat with flair,
Dances on shelves without a care.
Listen closely, and you might just hear,
The yarns of a grandma, light as a deer.

Grandpa's old chair creaks in delight,
Sharing its wisdom in the dead of night.
The clock chimes a giggle, not quite a sound,
As echoes of laughter in shadows abound.

With every creak, with every moan,
A tapestry of life in the walls is sewn.
This house, a jester, with stories to spin,
Each tells a tale of the joy within.

Murmurs of the Living Past

Footsteps patter on a well-worn floor,
A ghostly dance of who lived before.
Chairs argue softly about who sits where,
While the spoons gossip without a care.

Windows chuckle, seeing the deluge,
Of past lives painted in every refuse.
Doors creak low, like secrets in jest,
Whispering moments of joy and pest.

A vase of petunias shares tales of cheer,
While curtains flutter, lending an ear.
Old clocks tick in a rhythm so strange,
Counting the laughs as times start to change.

In each crack and chip, there's laughter to see,
Jokes passed through ages, just wait and agree.
The spirit of fun fills the walls with a grin,
Murmurs of yore invite you to spin.

The Language of Shifting Floors

Upon these planks, a chatter unfolds,
With ticklish footsteps, both timid and bold.
Each creak is a word, each squeak tells a tale,
Of little ones scrambling, of cats on the prowl.

Carpets giggle at the dance of the shoes,
While scattered toys share long-forgotten blues.
A jiggle, a jangle, the floors spring to life,
Echoing laughter, both sweet and rife.

With every step, the rhythm grows bright,
As toddlers chase dragons that glide out of sight.
Mismatched slippers may sometimes collide,
Turning the floor into a wild fun ride.

As night draws near, the floors start to whisper,
Enticing the dreams, becoming the drifter.
One last jiggle, before morning arrives,
In this playful realm, joy always thrives.

Dialogues Beneath the Eaves

Up high within the rafters, they meet,
Squirrels debate over leftover sweet.
Starlings squawk tales of adventures bright,
While cobwebs critique with a playful light.

Beneath the eaves, secrets resume,
Chattering voices sweep away gloom.
A creaky old beam joins in the fun,
As shadows dance 'til the day is done.

Bats have a laugh, flitting to and fro,
Trading old jingles no human could know.
Every tumble and flutter adds to the glee,
Creating a symphony, wild and free.

So here in this nest, laughter drifts high,
Echoing joy as the daylight flies by.
Under eaves above, let the fables ascend,
In a world full of voices, there's always a friend.

The Quiet Symphony of Everyday Life

In the kitchen, pots may clank,
While the dog gives a sneaky prank.
The cat sips tea, with delicate grace,
As grandma's slippers quicken the pace.

The toaster pops, in a playful feat,
And socks hide well, creating a cheat.
A laugh escapes when the fridge door swings,
As dinner dances on imaginary strings.

The clock ticks loud like a drummer's beat,
While kids play tag, oh, what a treat!
A distant yell over spilled juice flies,
And the radio bursts out in silly cries.

Here in this space, where chaos reigns,
Each echo brings back familiar strains.
For in the laughter and gentle hum,
Life's little symphony is never done.

Heartbeats of Forgotten Histories

Old portraits gaze from dusty walls,
Whispering tales of epic falls.
A grandpa's wig on the chair's edge lean,
As a ghost tries to learn how to clean.

The stories swirl like autumn leaves,
In every corner, a past that grieves.
Yet laughter erupts when uncle slips,
With tales that echo through countless quips.

Monocles glare from the shadows so bright,
A book on the shelf mutters, 'What's right?'
The echo of laughter, a booming clank,
Where time seems stuck in a laughing prank.

In the attic where secrets abide,
A thousand voices, not one can hide.
Each heartbeat calls, urging the past,
In this circus of memories, endless and vast.

The Cadence of Close Encounters

At the edge of the yard, the beans try to sprout,
A neighbor shouts, 'You've got a route!'
With aliens buzzing, telling their tales,
While the cat just stares, and wags its tails.

Two kids debate who's faster than light,
As the postman swoops by, a comical sight.
The ball sailed high, then fell on the lawn,
Finding a dog that's plotting till dawn.

In the shadows, a raccoon peeks wide,
As strangers share smiles, in laughter they confide.
The moon winks down, knows all of their quests,
While crickets chirp to offer some zest.

Close encounters of a laughter-filled kind,
In each strange meeting, joy intertwined.
With every chuckle, a moment to share,
In this funny world, filled with love and care.

A Collection of Silenced Expressions

The fish in the tank, with noses a-press,
Glance at secrets none would confess.
Outside, a gnome with a hat too grand,
Whispers about things he can't quite understand.

A broom in the corner, a grumpy old chap,
Wonders if it's time for a nap or a map.
While the curtains sway in a breezy dance,
They giggle softly at every chance.

A vase of flowers, who just can't disagree,
Ponder the meaning of life over tea.
While the rug rolls out, a comedy act,
In this sweet chaos, there's no need to crack.

In every silence, an untold jest,
With smiles exchanged, this house knows best.
From the cobwebbed corners to sparkling lights,
A collection of whispers, turning wrongs into rights.

Chronicles of the Hearth

In the corner, a cat gives a sigh,
While the toaster pops with a joyful cry.
The fridge hums low, a bass-like beat,
As the kettle whistles, a tune so sweet.

Grandpa's stories echo off the wall,
He swears he caught a fish, ten feet tall.
A ghostly laugh floats through the air,
As Auntie Jane claims she once danced on a bear.

The dog barks loudly, joining the fun,
While the vacuum roars like a monster on the run.
A chorus of chaos, a symphony bright,
In this lively home, every day feels right.

The Soundtrack of Sweet Remembrance

Clatter of dishes becomes a band,
While kids play drums with a spatula in hand.
Laughter rings clear, like bells in the air,
As Uncle Joe tries to juggle, unaware.

Whispers of secrets dance past the door,
While old vinyl crackles, bringing back lore.
A tickle of giggles, a dash of delight,
Like fireflies twinkling in the soft night light.

Echoes of antics, sweet versus sour,
Each corner alive with laughter's power.
We sing out of tune, but who really cares?
In our world of echoes, we banish all scares.

Names Carved in Air

Candles flicker with tales never told,
As shadows dance bold, shimmering gold.
Is that Grandma's voice calling from the shelf?
Or just the old clock trying to tell of itself?

The dust motes glide, like whispers in flight,
Carrying names through the heart of the night.
Each corner a story, a laugh, or a shout,
With every new guest, the joy grows about.

Crumbs drop from fingers like secret confessions,
While everyone's plotting with wild obsessions.
A fruitcake that wobbles is all the rage,
As we carve our names on this unwritten page.

Threads of Unseen Conversations

In the attic, a hat sits, collecting old schemes,
While slippers argue about whose turn to dream.
The curtains gossip about the weather outside,
As the shoes on the floor launch a dance full of pride.

Murmurs of memories weave through the hall,
As shadows join in, answering the call.
"Who let the dog out?" echoes from the kitchen,
While pots start to clap, all too proud to be glitchin'.

The clock chimes in, with a tick and a tock,
As family tales tumble like a vintage clock.
We laugh 'til we cry, we dance 'til we're sore,
In this whirlpool of laughter, who could ask for more?

The Chime of Shared Experience

In the kitchen, pots do dance,
A spoon fell down, missed its chance.
Laughter echoes off the walls,
While the cat still makes its calls.

Every cupboard holds a tale,
Of burnt toast and a ship's great sail.
We toast to mishaps, drink in cheer,
As Aunt Sue's fish was never clear.

From the garden, voices beam,
Silly jokes, a wild dream.
A gnome dares knock upon the door,
While Uncle Jim spills cider on the floor.

At dusk, we gather round to play,
Board games loud, all the way.
With wild bets, and sharing pies,
Every day is a sweet surprise.

Where Memories Gather

Dusty frames, old jokes fly high,
Grandpa's chin, a wobbly eye.
Family trees, branches entwine,
Stories mixed like homemade wine.

Chairs creak, as laughter rings,
Tales of dogs and daring flings.
In each nook, a giggle gleams,
Echoes dance like childhood dreams.

Cookies crumble, crumbs like rain,
Nana swears she'll never strain.
Cousins huddle in the hall,
Creating chaos with their brawl.

And when the sun begins to fade,
The magic of the day is made.
We pack the noise and save the fun,
A tapestry we're woven from.

Ghosts of Laughter and Grief

In the attic, whispers sigh,
Old shoes shuffle, asking why.
The grandma ghost starts to tease,
While we munch on stale cheese.

Echoes bubble from the past,
A dance that blooms, shadows cast.
With every giggle, a tear's trace,
Reminds us of a warm embrace.

In the parlor, spirits blend,
With every story that won't end.
Gramps' bad jokes float through the air,
But we forgive him; it's quite rare.

Though laughter stings, we hold it dear,
For every ghost brings us near.
Together still, we freely roam,
Creating joy, in our home.

Threads of Connected Lives

A tapestry of quirky threads,
Stitched with laughter, love, and spreads.
Each tale is woven, bright and bold,
In a rhythm, a pattern unfold.

From Uncle's bagpipes, sweet and loud,
To sister's quirks that make us proud.
We dance in circles, a silly spree,
Twisting tales like spaghetti.

Neighbors peek through curtains, grinned,
At drama plays we unrestrained.
Potlucks filled with fun surprise,
As Auntie shows up in her disguise.

These threads, they twine, they bounce with glee,
A web of mishaps, just you and me.
In every knot, a shared delight,
Connecting lives in love's own light.

A Melodic Embrace

In the living room, a sock does dance,
While the fridge hums a curious romance.
The cat croons soft to a pair of shoes,
As the clock ticks in sync with all the blues.

The dishes clatter their own sweet song,
While the chairs creak a tale, not too long.
With laughter echoing off the walls,
Even the wallpaper seems to have calls.

Each corner hides a giggling ghost,
Who jokes and jests, and loves to boast.
The curtains sway, with secrets they keep,
As the playful shadows start to leap.

In a friendly chorus, they all agree,
Home's not just walls, but this grand symphony.
With every corner humming their part,
A melodic embrace warms the heart.

Chants of the Resilient

In the hallway, shoes all squeak and sigh,
As the dust bunnies plot their sly reply.
The vacuum sings, a comedic hum,
While mice in the pantry play the drum.

Spoons in the drawer rattle with cheer,
While the kettle whistles songs, oh so clear.
The couch joins in with a creaky beat,
Cheering up all who dare take a seat.

Echoes of laughter brawl through the air,
As mirrors reflect the funny affair.
Even the fridge shares a joke or two,
About that pickle jar, proud and blue.

Together they chant, through thick and thin,
In this quirky home, where giggles begin.
The voices unite, both bold and new,
In the rhythm of life, that feels like a brew.

The Unsung Saga

Once a chair, claimed by a cat so sly,
Always plotting while humans pass by.
The table's stories, covered in dust,
Of spills and meals, in memories we trust.

In the silence of night, the walls start to chat,
About a lost sock and a chubby cat.
While spoons from the drawer engage in a fight,
On who's made the most noise in the night.

The floors grumble tales of stomping feet,
And whispers of crumbs that make them feel sweet.
High up on shelves, mug clinks with glee,
Sharing mishaps of coffee, oh, what a spree!

So here lie the secrets, right under our nose,
In each silly tale, life brightly glows.
With laughter resounding in every nook,
The unsung saga, from each corner, took.

Stories Behind Closed Doors

Behind every door, a tale does unfold,
From whispers of secrets, to snippets of bold.
The closet chuckles, with shoes in a fling,
While old suits remember the dances they'd bring.

The bathroom's a stage, with bubbles that sing,
As brushes and combs do their offering.
Toilet paper rolls in a dramatic twist,
Each square holds a story that simply can't miss.

In the pantry, jars clink their own little jive,
While cookies wait patiently, looking alive.
The spice rack snickers with sizzling zest,
In the kitchen's embrace, flavors feel blessed.

Join the laughter from rooms far and near,
With doors that conceal, yet celebrate cheer.
These stories abound, in every facade,
Behind closed doors, life's a mirthful charade.

The Symphony of Silent Echoes

In the corner, the cat's fur flies,
While the parrot mocks and replies.
The goldfish swims with a flashy glee,
Bubbles popping like a symphony.

Socks in the hallway, a wearer's disgrace,
Each pet's a witness; they hold their place.
The fridge hums softly a tune so light,
As the pizza box moans about last night.

A raccoon rummages with daring moves,
Turning trash into dance, oh how it grooves!
In this grand stage where laughter swells,
Every critter knows their roles so well.

Cameos of chaos blend in the fun,
When the humans arrive, oh what have they spun?
This merry symphony, wild and loud,
In this space of laughter, we're all so proud!

Reflections in Dusty Mirrors

A mirror laughs in the afternoon light,
It reflects the cat, quite a silly sight.
With the dust on the glass, stories unfold,
Of brushes and whispers and tales of old.

The dog wears a hat, thinking it's chic,
As the mirror chuckles, sneaky and meek.
The plants gossip softly, leaves all a-flutter,
While the clock ticks time, making humor stutter.

In the quiet corners, the shadows partake,
Of mishaps and laughter, they dance and shake.
A sock in the hallway recalls its long trip,
While the rug plays a tune, doing a flip!

With reflections of joy, absurd and unclear,
The dusty old mirror holds every cheer.
In this space of echoes, both silly and true,
We find our own laughter, just waiting for you!

The Tapestry of Unheard Tales

Threads of colors weave oh so bright,
In the fabric of life, each stitch a delight.
The couch recalls secrets, it's seen and it's told,
Of family meetings, and pranks, brave and bold.

The rug whispers softly of sticky feet,
Each pattern a memory, none can defeat.
The curtains shake hands with the breeze outside,
And giggle at shadows that swirl and glide.

Old photographs smirk from inside their frames,
Capturing hilarity, forgotten names.
The walls hold the laughter, both bright and unplanned,
In this woven snare, life's magic is grand.

In this tapestry woven of jests and of cheer,
Each thread holds a chuckle, a giggle, a sneer.
Among all the tales that dance in delight,
We gather the laughter, both day and night!

Footsteps of Echoing Souls

Footsteps shuffle with a comedic thud,
From a tall chair, the dog gives a shrug.
They hop and they skip, with a wily stance,
In the rhythm of chaos, we join in the dance.

The hallway knows secrets, it creaks and it sighs,
While the fridge joins in with its deep, distant cries.
The cat rolls its eyes, unimpressed by the show,
Yet leaps at the shadows, seeking a foe.

Every squeak of a shoe tells a joke from the past,
The laughter erupts, oh how it is cast!
In this parade of misfits, we wobble and sway,
With echoes of joy leading the way.

The footsteps tell stories, both funny and spry,
In every corner, their giggles comply.
As we traverse this playful abode,
The sounds of our souls weave a whimsical road!

www.ingramcontent.com/pod-product-compliance
Lightning Source LLC
Chambersburg PA
CBHW060141230426
43661CB00003B/515